Cocktails FOR A Crowd

More than 40 Recipes for Making Popular Drinks in Party-Pleasing Batches

Kara Newman

PHOTOGRAPHS BY TERI LYN FISHER

CHRONICLE BOOKS

SAN FRANCISCO

Library of Congress Cataloging-in-Publication Data available.

ISBN 978-1-4521-0949-7

Manufactured in China

Designed by **VANESSA DINA**
Prop styling by **TERI LYN FISHER**
Props provided by **BAMBU**
Food styling by **JENNY PARK**
Typesetting by **DC TYPE**

Pimm's is a registered trademark of The Pimm's Company.

10 9 8 7 6 5 4 3 2 1

Chronicle Books LLC
680 Second Street
San Francisco, California 94107
WWW.CHRONICLEBOOKS.COM

Dedicated to Maddy and Rowana

ACKNOWLEDGMENTS

Like every book, this one was made with the assistance of a crowd. Thank you to everyone.

The "dream team" at Chronicle Books, including Vanessa Dina, Doug Ogan, Claire Fletcher, Marie Oishi, Bill LeBlond, Sarah Billingsley, David Hawk, Peter Perez, and Tera Killip, as well as copy editor Jasmine Star.

My editors at *Wine Enthusiast Magazine,* for their kind understanding and support as I worked on this book, especially Susan Kostrzewa, Tim Moriarty, Joe Czerwinski, Alexis Korman, Marina Vataj, and Lauren Buzzeo.

All the amazing bartenders who contributed recipes and insight: Jason Asher, Scott Baird, Corey Bunnewith, Martin Cate, Kevin Diedrich, Tasha Garcia-Gibson, Charles Joly, Ryan Maybee, Jim Meehan, Stephen Savage, Eric Seed, Colin Shearn, and Kelley Swenson.

The drink testers, who provided thoughtful feedback under the guise of a rowdy cocktail party: Tim Braswell, Jennifer Corrao, Limor Elkayam and friend, Suzanne Fass, Aileen Goldstein, Nick Jackson, Chester Jankowski, Carolyn Karver-Wesenberg, Alexis Korman, Nora Maynard, Georgette Moger, Alex Moir, Keith Morton, Ian Nathan, Caroline Pacht, Sami Plotkin, Meryl Rosofsky, Robert Silverman, and Mel Wesenberg. Thanks for letting me test the limits of your goodwill—and your livers.

The proud-to-be-cocktail-geeks of the Mixoloseum online community, who provided a friendly sounding board and cheerfully boozy companionship during the long at-the-keyboard days. It was the next best thing to a being at a bar.

My extended family: Eliott and Naomi Newman; Jennifer and Madelyn Sendor; Alan and Sandy Silverman; and Joelle, Laurie, and Rowana Fay Miller—and especially my supportive and extremely tolerant husband, Robert Silverman, even though after this project he claims that he no longer drinks.

COOL CLASSIC PUNCHES PITCHERS PITCHERS TIKI TROPICAL

PUNCHES PITCHERS PITCHERS TIKI TIKI TROPICAL COOL CLASSIC

PUNCHES PITCHERS TIKI TIKI TROPICAL COOL CLASSIC

PUNCHES PITCHERS TIKI TROPICAL COOL CLASSIC PUNCHES

PITCHERS TIKI TROPICAL COOL CLASSIC PUNCHES PITCHERS

Contents

INTRODUCTION

I'd like to say that this book arose from my own experience as a perfect, unflappable hostess. But nothing could be further from the truth. I worry. I fuss. And worst of all, I'm the kind of person who traps myself behind the bar for the entire duration of a party, painstakingly measuring out every ounce of whiskey and squeezing juice, one lemon wedge at a time—in short, making individual drinks in what feels like slow motion.

It helps to know that this afflicts the pros, too, sometimes. As a cocktail and spirits writer, I attend a lot of events where cocktails are served to large groups: bar openings, product launches, cocktail conferences, and the like. Sometimes I see the bartenders struggling to keep up with demand, mixing and shaking frenetically while the parched crowd gathers around the bar area, five and six people deep, waiting for drinks inevitably mixed with flop sweat.

That sounds a lot like how I feel when I'm playing bartender at a party.

But it doesn't have to be that way. And in fact, at most professional events, the drinks service appears smooth and calm (at least from where I'm standing), and the cocktails are usually amazing. The bartenders actually smile, the drinks flow easily, and the guests have a great time. What makes the difference?

I've been asking mixologists, conducting interviews and asking for their best tips and drink recipes. Their responses generally fall into two categories: First, choose the right cocktails to serve to a large group—drinks that are easy to prepare on the spot or that can be made in advance and self-served but will hold up over the course of an evening. In some cases, the bartenders provided their thoughts on how to tweak standard cocktails to make them more appropriate for serving to a crowd. Second, do as much advance preparation as possible. This includes implementing good *mise en place* at the bar (having ingredients and equipment set up in advance; see page 14), batching drinks to make larger quantities, and using professional serving techniques. Some of the tips pleasantly surprised me, such as adding water to home-bottled drinks to approximate the effect of melting ice in a cocktail. Others, such as *mise en place*, struck a common-sense chord, a feeling of "Now why didn't I think of that before?"

There's no reason why the techniques the professionals employ can't be used for events hosted at home, whether that means a dinner party for eight (the minimum number of people constituting a "crowd," my editors have decreed) or a backyard barbecue for forty.

Interest in and recipes for cocktails suitable for serving to a crowd seem to be growing rapidly. From punches to pitchers and from classic drinks writ large to tiki concoctions intended for sizable groups, such as the Scorpion Bowl (page 70), there are numerous recipes for those who don't want to spend all night mixing individual drinks at parties. In this book I've aspired to provide the "best in breed" of these drinks. I've also smoothed out some of the cocktail math involved in scaling up these tipples. The recipes in this book use both fluid ounces (the preferred measurement used by jigger-wielding bartenders) and tablespoons, cups, and so on for liquid ingredients, allowing you to use whichever measures you prefer. The total

volume of each recipe also is provided to make it easier for you to plan what vessels to use for mixing and serving drinks.

Speaking of vessels for serving drinks, feel free to stray from those suggested in this book. Take cues from the growing ranks of bars that serve cocktails in a variety of creative containers: glorious cut-glass or antique pewter bowls, carafes, decanters, *gallones* (a large Italian mixing glass), teapots, samovars, and even fishbowls and small fountains. You might seek inspiration from items lurking in dark corners of your cabinets—new life for that old fondue pot, perhaps?

Of course, there was only one way to field-test the drinks in this book: throw a party! So I did, setting out punches, pitchers, and home-bottled cocktails. I'm pleased to report that once guests arrived, I squeezed not a single lemon wedge. It was liberating to be out from behind the bar.

So go ahead—relax. Send out the invitations. The drinks for your next event are covered.

However, as for what to wear to the soirée? Sorry, you're on your own.

CHAPTER 1

THE Set-Up

Advice from Bartenders: How to Batch Great Cocktails

Every mixologist worth his or her shaker is trained to craft a delightful cocktail for one. But is it possible to duplicate that delight on a larger scale?

If you've ever been to one of the growing ranks of cocktail conferences, such as Tales of the Cocktail in New Orleans or the Manhattan Cocktail Classic in New York, you'll know the answer is a resounding *yes!* Every year, scores of talented bartenders flock to these conferences, where they go through the choreography of churning out great drinks for hundreds of cocktail enthusiasts at a go.

Behind the scenes, it's like watching a buzzing beehive: all those frenetic bartenders pouring out bottles from both hands into enormous buckets, stirring with giant spoons that resemble canoe oars, and dipping straws into the buckets to (hygienically) get a taste, and a taste, and yet another taste as they go. When the drink is deemed ready, it's decanted into dainty one-person servings that are garnished in a flash and delivered to the thirsty masses on serving trays. Despite the scale, each drink is held to the same standard as if it had been made individually.

In the industry, this scaling up of proportions and mixing drinks for large groups is referred to as "batching." And it isn't as simple as taking a favorite drink recipe and multiplying it by the number of tipplers.

I asked a number of seasoned bar pros to share how to batch great drinks. Here's the best of their advice.

MEASURE ACCURATELY, AND USE THE RIGHT TOOL FOR THE JOB.

"Punch is a fun way to batch for a large group, but you still need to measure accurately and make sure your measurements are correct. I use clear Oxo measuring cups with measurements on the inside. They're really handy and pour nicely. Batching with a jigger would be a pain." —*Ryan Maybee, bartender and co-owner, Manifesto, Kansas City*

BEWARE OF "EXPANDING" FLAVORS.

"The strong flavors of some spirits expand, so you should use less; for example, fernet, absinthe, maraschino liqueur, and Green Chartreuse. For large batches, start with half as much as the original recipe calls for, then stir and taste it, and add a little more as needed." —*Jim Meehan, managing partner, PDT, New York*

USE TEA TO FLAVOR PUNCHES.

"Tea doesn't get enough play as an ingredient. Especially for a punch, it's historically accurate yet awesomely delicious. It can help smooth out some of the mistakes you might make in other steps. If it's too tart, add tea (and more water). Too sweet? Same thing. The tannins balance out the sweetness. It's also a way to create more complexity. Tea is where it's at. . . . It's in most of our punches for a reason." —*Colin Shearn, general manager, the Franklin Mortgage & Investment Co., Philadelphia*

KEEP IT SIMPLE AND TASTE OFTEN.

"You don't want to go over the top with ingredients. Taste it. If you batch a recipe for a single drink to serve a lot of people, the balance gets off, citrus to sugar. Keep tasting it every time you increase the batch." —*Kevin Diedrich, bar manager, Jasper's Corner Tap, San Francisco*

CONSIDER THE COLOR.

"If you get a small drink on the rocks and it's murky brown, no problem. If you get a punch and it's from a trough of murky brown? Not sexy. Even a garnish won't save it. I always think about the tonality of the drink, even if it means not using an ingredient I wanted." —*Scott Baird, founding partner of Bon Vivants cocktail consultancy and bartender, Trick Dog, San Francisco*

MUDDLE AND THEN STRAIN.

"Muddled flavors can get too strong. I muddle the herbs, fruits, or other ingredients with gin (or other spirits), and then let it sit. Then I strain it. . . . You get the flavor, it doesn't continue to infuse, and it's easier to serve for large batches." —*Jim Meehan*

THINK ABOUT THE STRENGTH AND AMOUNT OF BOOZE.

"Without anyone moderating the size of pours, it's easy for guests to drink more than they intended, especially with very strong and very delicious drinks. . . . I might put out smaller pitchers and replenish. It's not the friendliest thing to do to a party, but it's too easy to get sloppy, and it's not the guest's fault." —*Scott Baird*

USE CITRUS WITH CARE.

"I prefer to use older juice—meaning a few hours old, or even a day old—for a large group. It oxidizes and the acidity is tamer, rather than really bright. I would juice in the morning and then use it at night. You can barely tell the difference, but it works.

"For batching, I prefer cocktails that don't really need sugar or citrus. Otherwise, they will eventually separate and you'll lose the freshness and quality of the cocktail. You can stir every thirty minutes to make sure nothing is settling, but that defeats the purpose of making it fast and accessible." —*Kevin Diedrich*

TAKE CONTROL OF THE DILUTION—NO ONE WANTS A WATERED-DOWN DRINK.

"For citrus-based drinks, which are typically shaken, my rule of thumb is the ice dilutes the drink by 25 to 30 percent. Count up all the ounces in the drink, multiply it by the number of servings, and add 25 percent water. I put it in the fridge in the morning, let it get cold, and that evening I just throw it into a pitcher.

"For a stirred cocktail, I like to add ice and then stir it and taste it. When it hits the right amount of dilution, I strain the ice out.

"Punches are different, because they typically dilute at their own rate, as a large block of ice melts. I just build the drink, and it evolves as it goes, from

really intense to a little diluted. Most people will drink it before it gets too diluted."
—*Jason Asher, head mixologist, Young's Market, Scottsdale*

"At events, we serve the Tipsy Palmer (page 58) in big urns we've purchased from Pottery Barn. We'll put bright yellow lemons in the bottom part, and the brown tea in the tall glass cylinder on top. It's simple, it looks great, and people can serve themselves. We do a fair amount of catering, and places that have self-serve bars are the most successful. That way, people don't feel weird about going back for seconds, and they don't make a mess, so that's good for the host." —*Stephen Savage, general manager and beverage director, Tipsy Parson, New York*

"With garnishes, I always wait until the last minute. I build drinks first thing in the morning, and then right before service I do the garnishes: lemon, orange peel, fresh herbs. Do it too early and it all gets weird.

"If you're batching a drink that has an effervescent portion (like soda or tonic), add it at the time of service."
—*Jason Asher*

Why *Mise en Place* Is Your Best Friend

Does this scenario sound familiar? The first guests are knocking at the door, but you aren't quite ready for the party. The bar isn't set up! You can't find your left shoe! You're feeling frazzled, and that's no way to start off a fun evening.

Exhale. It happens to everyone. It certainly happens to me. But it won't be a big deal if your *mise en place* is good to go.

Mise en place (pronounced meez-ahn-plahs) is a French culinary term that means "putting in place." In a kitchen or bar setting, it's the practice of preparing food or drink ahead of time as much as possible so everything is ready to be combined and then setting all the ingredients and equipment needed in their appropriate places. If you're planning to entertain a group, *mise en place* is your best friend.

Go to a good bar early in the evening, and you'll find the bartender in the process of the daily *mise en place* ritual. For example, you may see bartenders squeezing citrus juice so they won't have to slow down to squeeze lemons for every individual drink later on. You might find others painstakingly cutting dozens of garnishes or trimming bunches of mint into sprigs sized perfectly for individual drinks. But beyond just cutting and trimming, *mise en place* extends to setting the garnishes aside in compartments within easy reach or arranging the sprigs jauntily in a glass with water, keeping them fresh and bright and ready to go. Then, when it's go time at the bar, drinks can be made fluidly, speedily, and well.

Home bartenders can benefit from *mise en place* too. This is less important when you're making drinks for one or two people. Who cares if you need to squeeze a lemon on the spot or hunt for that bottle of gin? But when you're planning cocktails for a crowd, the secret to effortless entertaining is planning ahead. Figure out exactly which liquors you'll need and how much of each, and also the amounts of mixers, ice, and garnishes. Also consider tools and glassware. And don't forget your cleanup gear, such as dish towels, paper towels, and trash bins. (If a sink isn't in easy reach, many bartenders recommend one trash bin for ice and liquids and a second receptacle for garbage.) Measure out and prepare your ingredients as much as possible and make sure everything is conveniently within reach, whether you're playing bartender or setting up an area where guests can serve themselves. Many of the drinks in this book can be put together in their entirety ahead of time.

Another aspect of *mise en place* is indicating to guests what's expected of them. If you're behind the bar, that makes it obvious: You'll be explaining and pouring as you go along. But if you'd rather be socializing than making drinks, take a minute to write the name of each drink on a separate index card, along with a note about what's in the drink. This will spare you from having to explain the ingredients repeatedly. Plus, those with allergies or, say, a post-bender aversion to tequila will thank you. If you expect guests to do some assembly, jot

down instructions, such as "1. Shake. 2. Pour into a glass. 3. Garnish with a lemon peel." One bartender interviewed for this book even suggested printing a photo of the finished drink and displaying it to let guests know what their drink should look like.

If this seems like common sense, congratulations—you're ahead of the game. If not, consider cocktail *mise en place* for your next gathering. When those first guests knock on the door, you'll be able to calmly point them to the bar, where they can happily fix a drink. They might not even notice that you're only wearing one shoe.

Equipment

A wide range of serving vessels are specified in the recipes in this book, usually selected with a mind toward showcasing the drink to best advantage; keeping it chilled or warm, as appropriate; and, in some cases, for historical accuracy. If you don't have the "right" glasses, don't worry; just use what seems to fit the drink best. Here's a guide to the glassware I call for:

- CHAMPAGNE FLUTE: A tall, narrow stemmed wineglass, intended to give bubbly drinks less surface area so the carbonation lasts as long as possible. Wineglasses or goblets may be substituted.
- COLLINS GLASS: A tall glass with straight vertical sides and plenty of room for ice, named for the Tom Collins cocktail. They typically hold 10 to 14 ounces (1¼ to 1¾ cups). Highball glasses may be substituted.
- COUPE: A stemmed glass with a rounded, saucerlike bowl, commonly used for classic cocktails. Martini glasses may be substituted.
- FOOTED MUG: A mug usually made of tempered glass and with a handle, and frequently used for hot drinks; also known as an Irish coffee mug. Regular coffee mugs may be substituted.
- HIGHBALL GLASS: The most common bar glass, with straight vertical sides, and usually holding 8 to 12 ounces (1 to 1½ cups). It is used for everything from Bloody Marys to gin and tonics. Although slightly larger, Collins glasses may be substituted.

- MARGARITA GLASS: A curvy stemmed glass typically used for margaritas and daiquiris. Standard martini glasses may be substituted.
- MARTINI GLASS: A stemmed glass with a V-shaped bowl, and the classic vessel for any drink served without ice—but especially a martini!
- OLD-FASHIONED GLASS: A short glass with straight vertical sides that typically holds 4 to 8 ounces (½ to 1 cup). It is the standard glass used for drinks mixed with ice.
- PUNCH GLASS: A cup that may or may not have handles and that may be made of glass or decorative materials. Teacups or old-fashioned glasses may be substituted.
- TIKI MUG: A whimsical vessel that comes in a wide range of shapes and sizes—the more garish, the better! While most tiki mugs are sized for one serving (usually comparable to a highball glass), scorpion bowls usually hold 20 ounces (2½ cups), and volcano bowls may hold from 32 to 48 ounces (4 to 6 cups), which is comparable to many punch bowls. However, these are rough guidelines, and the sizes of scorpion bowls and volcano bowls can vary widely. Be that as it may, one standard remains: They're sized for sharing.
- WINE GOBLET OR WINEGLASS: An assuredly familiar vessel. A standard white wineglass holds from 6 to 12 ounces (¾ to 1½ cups), while larger and more rounded red wineglasses may hold anywhere from 8 to 24 ounces (1 to 3 cups).

Beyond glassware, making and serving cocktails doesn't require much special equipment. You probably already have most of what you need. Here's a quick rundown of the tools and equipment specified in the recipes in this book:

- BLENDER: For crushing ice and blending frozen drinks.
- FINE-MESH SIEVE: Good for straining herbs and other solids from infusions.
- HAWTHORNE STRAINER: A flat strainer equipped with a spring coil so it fits neatly into a mixing glass to prevent ice from falling into a drink. For large drinks made in pitchers, a large wooden spoon can be used to hold back ice, or you may wish to pour through a fine-mesh sieve.
- INFUSION JAR: Large Mason-style jars with spouts at the bottom. Although not obligatory at all, they can be useful for making and serving sangrias and other infused drinks with ease.
- JIGGER: Available in a variety of sizes, and often double-sided, with a different measure on each end. They are excellent for measuring out ounces, but be sure to check how many ounces your jigger holds before using it.
- LONG-HANDLED SPOON: Perfect for reaching down into the bottom of a mixing glass or pitcher to stir thoroughly.
- MEASURING CUP OR GLASS: If possible, select a glass with measures for both cups and ounces.
- MEASURING SPOONS: Measures for teaspoons and tablespoons come in handy for bitters, spices, extracts, and other ingredients used in small amounts.
- MIXING GLASS: A vessel specifically designed for stirring drinks with ice. Although any large glass or pitcher can be used for this purpose, many mixing glasses have spouts that make for easy pouring.
- MUDDLER: A tool somewhat like a mini baseball bat, usually with a blunt or rounded edge at one end. It is used for crushing herbs, spices, or other ingredients. The back of a spoon also can be used in a pinch.

Ice for a Crowd

Although most drinks can be chilled with standard ice cubes, it's worth mastering two additional ice formats: block ice for punch bowls and crushed ice for tiki drinks. Another option—one that's a bit of a novelty—is to make shaped cubes using silicone ice molds.

PUNCH BOWL ICE

Don't use ice cubes for punches; they will melt quickly and water down the punch. Instead, use large blocks of ice, which will melt slowly over the course of an evening.

Since this ice will eventually mix with the drinks, consider using bottled or filtered water if the quality of your tap water isn't great. For crystal-clear ice, use distilled or boiled water. When selecting a container for freezing the ice, the key is go as big as possible while still leaving room in the punch bowl to maneuver the ladle.

SIMPLE PUNCH BOWL ICE: At least a day in advance, pour water into disposable aluminum loaf pans, filling them about halfway, or disposable aluminum pie pans and freeze until completely firm. When you're ready to serve the punch, peel the pan away. Alternatively, use a bowl to create rounded ice. Run the bottom of the bowl under hot water briefly to release the ice.

DECORATIVE PUNCH BOWL ICE: For more decorative ice, use a Bundt pan or tube pan. At least a day in advance, fill the pan with water and freeze until completely firm. When you're ready to serve, run the bottom of the pan under hot water briefly to release the ice.

TINTED OR FRUITED ICE: Another option for decorative punch bowl ice is to mix the water with fruit juice or fruit, such as pineapple rings or cranberries, before freezing. Just be aware that as the ice melts, the juice or fruit will become part of the punch, and this can affect the flavor.

FANCY PUNCH BOWL ICE: Making this ice requires a couple of freezing sessions, but it can be worth the effort for events where you want to impress:

1. Cut fruit, such as lemons or oranges, into thin slices, or use small, whole fruits such as berries. Herbs, such as mint or rosemary, or edible flower petals are also an option.

2. Arrange the sliced fruit, herbs, or flower petals in an overlapping pattern around the outer edge of the pan. Set berries along the bottom of the pan. Pour in enough water to hold the decorations in place against the outside of the pan or to submerge fruit on the bottom of the pan—about ½ inch of water. Freeze until firm, about 2 hours.

3. Fill the pan with cold water, completely submerging the fruit. Freeze until solid, usually at least 4 hours, before using.

HOW MUCH ICE?

YOU'VE HEARD THE HOST'S MAXIM: *You can never have too much ice.* But is there any way to determine how much is enough? Portland bartender Kelley Swenson has a simple formula: For each 750 milliliters of cocktail (the size of a standard bottle of liquor), he allots 7 pounds of ice. "And then I add extra," Swenson says. "You can never have too much ice, and it is devastating to run out."

HERE'S THE COCKTAIL MATH: 750 ml equals about 3¼ cups. So once you've figured out which cocktails you'll be serving and the volumes you plan to make, you can calculate the amount of ice you'll need (keeping in mind that punches should be chilled using solid blocks of ice in the bowl, not ice cubes). Obviously, not all that ice will go into pitchers or other bulk containers. Some will go into cups, glasses, or cocktail shakers, or into buckets to help keep bottles cold.

HERE'S ANOTHER TIP FROM KELLEY SWENSON: If at all possible, don't use bags of ice from convenience stores, since that ice may have "off" flavors. "I prefer to make ice myself or build a relationship with a store or bar that can sell good ice to me."

CRUSHED ICE

Crushed ice is the polar opposite of long-lasting punch bowl ice. In tiki-style drinks and other potent libations, its purpose is to melt quickly and dilute the drink. It shouldn't be made ahead of time. Crush it as described below, scoop it into the glasses, pour the drinks over the ice, and serve immediately.

Sure, you can crush ice in a blender, but doing it by hand is a great way for you or a friend to release a little tension—and it also makes for an even more dynamic and memorable gathering. To crush ice by hand, scoop it into a canvas bag (the Lewis Ice Bag is specially made for this task) or a plastic zip-top freezer bag (squeeze out all the air before closing it, or it will pop when you crush the ice). Beat the bag with a rolling pin, a large muddler, or a meat pounder to crush the ice.

SILICONE ICE MOLDS

If you really want to go the extra mile, consider investing in silicone ice molds, which can be used to freeze ice into spheres or large cubes, both excellent for chilling spirit-forward cocktails such as Madison Avenue Manhattans (page 79), or a special Scotch you don't want to dilute too much. This type of ice is probably best for smallish groups and beverages where you'll only be using one or two ice spheres or cubes per drink.

Garnishes and Other Ingredients

As much as possible, make your garnishes ahead of time, then set them up next to the drinks they're intended to embellish. Some, such as maraschino cherries, brandied cherries, and pickled cocktail onions, must be made from 1 day to 2 weeks in advance. Most others, such as citrus garnishes, should be prepared shortly before serving time so they'll be as fresh as possible.

Maraschino Cherries
MAKES ABOUT 2 CUPS

Why buy dyed, flavorless maraschino cherries when they're so easy to assemble? The only hard part is waiting a couple of weeks while they marinate. Just one word of warning: Although I prefer to make this recipe with the cherries intact, pits and all, to add a subtle touch of almondlike flavor, many people don't care for pits in their maraschino cherries. If that includes you, go ahead and pit the cherries first.

1 pound ripe cherries, intact with stems and pits, washed well

16 to 24 ounces (2 to 3 cups) Luxardo maraschino liqueur

Put the cherries in a 2-quart glass jar or other glass container with a lid. Pour the liqueur over the cherries, adding enough to immerse the fruit (but note that they'll bob to the top of the liquid).

Cover and refrigerate for at least 2 weeks before using. Gently swirl the container every 2 to 3 days so all the cherries will be evenly immersed in the liqueur. Stored in a cool, dark place, the cherries will keep for about 1 month.

Brandied Cherries
MAKES ABOUT ¾ CUP

This is my go-to recipe when fresh cherries aren't available. Dried, pitted Bing cherries plump up when soaked in a spirits-based syrup. Adding a dash of almond or vanilla extract mimics the flavor usually imparted by the cherry pits.

½ cup sugar

4 ounces (½ cup) water

½ cup dried cherries

¼ teaspoon almond or vanilla extract

4 ounces (½ cup) brandy, bourbon, aged rum, or other brown spirits, plus more as needed

In a small saucepan, combine the sugar and water over medium-high heat. Cook, stirring constantly, until the sugar is dissolved and the syrup is boiling. Lower the heat to maintain a simmer, then stir in the cherries and almond extract. Simmer uncovered, stirring occasionally, until the liquid thickens to a light syrupy consistency, 5 to 7 minutes. Remove from the heat, stir in the brandy, and let cool to room temperature.

Transfer the cherries and liquid to a 1-quart glass jar or other glass container with a lid. Add more brandy if needed to cover the cherries. Covered and stored in the refrigerator, the cherries will keep for about 2 weeks.

PICKLED VEGETABLES

Look for jars of various pickled vegetables at farmers' markets and specialty markets; you can also find them in many regular supermarkets near the pickles. More unusual choices, such as pickled string beans or okra, can add extra color and crunch to martinis, Bloody Marys, and other drinks.

DIY Cocktail Onions
MAKES ABOUT ½ CUP

These savory, crunchy pickled onions are the classic garnish for a Gibson, but they also make fun bar snacks. To peel onions easily, try the blanching method: Boil them for a couple of minutes, then drain and transfer to an ice bath. Once the onions are cool enough to handle, cut off the root ends; the onions should squeeze right out of their skins.

8 ounces (1 cup) Champagne vinegar or sherry vinegar

⅓ cup sugar

½ tablespoon salt

½ teaspoon pickling spice

4 ounces pearl onions, peeled

Splash of dry vermouth

In a small saucepan, combine the vinegar, sugar, salt, and pickling spice. Bring to a boil over medium-high heat, stirring often. Lower the heat to maintain a simmer and add the onions. Cook, stirring occasionally, for about 5 minutes. Remove from the heat and let cool to room temperature.

Transfer the onions and liquid to a 1-quart glass jar or other glass container with a lid and add the vermouth. Refrigerate for at least 12 hours before using. Covered and stored in the refrigerator, the onions will keep for about 1 month.

STUFFED COCKTAIL OLIVES
Although stuffed olives couldn't be simpler to make, they add an unusual twist to martinis and Bloody Marys. Plus, making them yourself gives you the opportunity to experiment with different flavors to complement different drinks. Use green olives—and use your imagination when it comes to the fillings. That said, here are a few ideas to get you started: piquant blue cheese, roasted garlic cloves, folded scraps of prosciutto, or almonds.

CITRUS GARNISHES
In a variety of forms from wheels to twists, citrus garnishes are almost always the perfect accessory for a well-dressed drink. Prepare one garnish per glass, and do it as close to service time as you can manage.

WHEELS: Cut the ends off a lemon, lime, or orange and discard. Slice the fruit into rounds about ¼ inch thick. If the wheel will be perched on the edge of the glass, cut a slit from the center of the fruit to the outer peel.

HALF WHEELS: Cut citrus wheels in half to create semicircles. If the half wheel will be perched on the edge of the glass, cut a slit in the center of the cut edge.

WEDGES: For wedges, cut lemons or limes into quarters lengthwise. Cut oranges into eighths.

PEELS: Use a knife or vegetable peeler to cut a swath of zest from the fruit. Many bartenders encourage using the serving

glass for inspiration: Cut thin pieces of peel for graceful glassware like champagne flutes and wider pieces for sturdy vessels like old-fashioned glasses.

TWISTS: Use a knife or vegetable peeler to cut strips approximately 1 inch wide and 4 inches long from the fruit. Cut each strip lengthwise to produce narrow 4-inch strips about ½ inch wide. Wind each around your fingertip into a circle and secure with a toothpick. Cover the twists with a damp paper towel until service time. When you're ready to serve drinks, remove the toothpicks and discard. Gently pull the twists to unfurl them.

SWEETENING SYRUPS

Making syrups to sweeten cocktails (and iced coffee . . . and lemonade . . .) is an easy task, yet it goes a long way toward taking drinks to the next level.

Simple Syrup
MAKES ABOUT 1¼ CUPS

This basic simple syrup recipe can be used in a broad range of cocktails, and it can easily be customized by adding flavorings like spices, herbs, or tea (see Note).

1 cup sugar

8 ounces (1 cup) water

In a small saucepan, combine the sugar and water. Cook over medium-high heat, stirring constantly, until the sugar is dissolved. When the syrup starts to boil, lower the heat to maintain a simmer. Cook, stirring occasionally, for 10 minutes.

Remove from the heat and let cool to room temperature. Stored in a covered container in the refrigerator, the syrup will keep for about 1 month.

NOTE: If making a flavored syrup, for example, with herbs, add them after the sugar has dissolved. Leave the flavorings in the syrup until it cools to room temperature, then remove, straining the syrup if needed to remove any of the flavorings.

Honey Syrup
MAKES ABOUT 1½ CUPS

Although honey is a delightful flavoring, it's too thick and sticky to use easily in cocktails. But when thinned with hot water, it has a perfect consistency for pouring, measuring, and combining into creative drinks. Note that honey syrup should be stored at room temperature and used within a day; if refrigerated, it will separate or crystallize, so it's easier to make a fresh batch than attempt to rescue an old one.

6 ounces (¾ cup) honey

6 ounces (¾ cup) water

In a small saucepan, combine the honey and water and cook over low heat, stirring constantly, until thoroughly blended. Let cool to room temperature. Stored in a covered container at room temperature, the syrup will keep for about 24 hours.

Techniques

The techniques involved in making cock-tails are generally very straightforward. Here are just a couple of pointers that you may find useful.

HOW TO MUDDLE: Muddling is simply crushing ingredients, such as herbs or fruit. Put the ingredients to be muddled in a cocktail shaker or pitcher and use a mud-dler or wooden spoon to crush them and release their flavors and juices.

HOW TO SQUEEZE LARGE AMOUNTS OF CITRUS JUICE: You'll notice that many of the recipes in this book call for freshly squeezed lemon or lime juice, some-times as much as 16 ounces (2 cups) per recipe—and in one case 60 ounces (7½ cups)! Resist the urge to substitute bottled lemon or lime juice, which tends to have off flavors and simply won't do your cocktails justice. To strengthen your resolve, here are some tips on how to coax maximum juice from citrus with minimal effort. First, be aware that fruit at room temperature yields more juice than chilled fruit. If necessary, microwave the fruit for 10 seconds to warm it to room temperature and encourage it to release more juice. Second, invest in a handheld metal juice press. These hinged, two-piece tools come in several sizes, suitable for limes, lemons, and larger citrus fruits. They usually cost less than $20, and they make the job much easier. Of course, if your budget permits, a heavy-duty upright juice press or electric juicer makes it easier still.

CHAPTER II

THE

Recipes

PUNCHES

Truly, we are enjoying a golden age of punches. In addition to the many wonderful classics, like Fish House Punch, these days it seems like most bartenders have created new and wonderful libations designed to be served in a punch bowl. Some bars have signature punches or offer punch du jour.

In recent years, I've also been to a few punch parties, and if any drink format is perfect for home entertaining, this is it. The only "special" technique you'll need to learn is how to make punch bowl ice—big blocks of ice that will melt slowly in the drink (see page 20). So splurge on that gorgeous silver punch bowl, pour in the ingredients, add the ice, and go enjoy the party!

Raspberry Bellinis

SERVES 16
TOTAL VOLUME: ABOUT 11½ CUPS (WITHOUT ICE)

8 ounces (1 cup) elderflower liqueur (such as St-Germain)

8 ounces (1 cup) raspberry purée, homemade (see Note) or store-bought

Three 750-ml bottles (about 9½ cups) Prosecco or other sparkling white wine

1 ice block

Fresh raspberries, for garnish

Typically, Bellinis are made with peach purée. But it's hard to resist the bright pink of raspberries, especially when they're in season. This effervescent drink looks especially pretty in a cut-glass punch bowl with a block of ice floated in the center. Boiron brand raspberry purée is excellent in this punch; you may be able to find it in the freezer section at quality markets, and you can also purchase it online. Alternatively, you can make it from scratch to take advantage of tasty, peak-of-season berries.

In a punch bowl, combine the elderflower liqueur and raspberry purée and stir well.

Just before serving, pour in the Prosecco and stir gently. Add the ice.

To serve, ladle into champagne flutes or crystal punch glasses. Garnish with fresh raspberries, floated in the glass or speared on toothpicks.

NOTE: To make raspberry purée, combine 2 cups raspberries, 2 ounces (¼ cup) freshly squeezed lemon juice, and ¼ cup sugar in a blender or food processor and process until smooth. Strain through a fine-mesh sieve. Stored in a covered container in the refrigerator, the purée will keep for about 4 days.

Botanical Aperitif Punch

SERVES 8 TO 10
TOTAL VOLUME: ABOUT 4¾ CUPS (WITHOUT ICE)

10 ounces (1¼ cups) gin with a botanical profile

10 ounces (1¼ cups) Lillet Blanc

10 ounces (1¼ cups) Honey Syrup (page 26)

7 ounces (¾ cup plus 2 tablespoons) freshly squeezed lemon juice

1 ice block

Ground cinnamon, for garnish (optional)

Thanks to Corey Bunnewith, mixologist with Citizen Public House in Boston, for this recipe for a light, crisp drink that lives up to the "aperitif" in its name. It is neither too boozy nor too strongly flavored and makes for a great serve-yourself tipple before dinner. Use a dry gin here, preferably one with a botanical, floral profile. Although gin is essentially vodka infused with botanicals, some varieties have more pronounced flavors. Another great option is Square One Botanical, a rye vodka infused with fruits and herbs, including lemon verbena, rosemary, and coriander. Consider freezing whole cranberries, edible flowers, or other decorative elements into the ice block for more visual impact (see page 20).

In a punch bowl, combine the gin, Lillet Blanc, honey syrup, and lemon juice and stir until thoroughly blended. Add the ice.
    To serve, ladle into coupe or martini glasses and garnish with a dusting of cinnamon, if desired.

French 75 Punch

SERVES 8
TOTAL VOLUME: 7¾ CUPS (WITHOUT ICE)

16 ounces (2 cups) gin (preferably a London dry gin, such as Tanqueray)

8 ounces (1 cup) freshly squeezed lemon juice

6 ounces (¾ cup) Simple Syrup (page 26)

½ teaspoon orange bitters

32 ounces (4 cups) dry Champagne or other sparkling dry white wine, chilled

1 large ice block or several smaller blocks

8 orange wheels, for garnish

The French 75 is a classic cocktail usually made with cognac, though gin is sometimes substituted, and that's the spirit I call for in this recipe. It typically isn't served as a punch but works quite well in this format. Serve this fresh, fragrant variation at any occasion that calls for toasting, like a brunch or a bridal or baby shower.

A simple chunk of ice, such as one frozen in a loaf pan or bowl will suffice, but for a special, decorative touch, consider freezing orange wheels inside the ice (see page 20).

In a punch bowl, combine the gin, lemon juice, simple syrup, and bitters and stir until thoroughly blended.

Just before serving, pour in the Champagne and stir gently. Add the ice and garnish with the orange wheels.

To serve, ladle into punch glasses.

Alchemist Punch

SERVES 10 TO 12
TOTAL VOLUME: ABOUT 9½ CUPS (WITHOUT ICE)

10 ounces (1¼ cups) warm water

1½ ounces (3 tablespoons) honey

One 750-ml bottle (about 3¼ cups) Bénédictine

16 ounces (2 cups) mandarin purée, homemade (see Note) or store-bought

12 ounces (1½ cups) freshly squeezed lemon juice

3 tangerines, cut into wedges

2 lemons, sliced into wheels

2½ cups ice cubes

This visually stunning punch was created by the makers of Bénédictine, an herbal liqueur that, as legend has it, was originally brewed by monks. I've made this for several history-minded events, and I can assure you that with its striking bright orange color and the fruit floating in the bowl, it looks as if you've gone to a lot more trouble than you have. Borrow a silver punch bowl and a ladle, and you'll have instant class in a glass. Boiron brand mandarin orange purée is excellent in this punch; you may be able to find it in the freezer section at quality markets, and you can also purchase it online. Alternatively, you can make it from scratch.

In a pitcher that holds at least 11 cups, combine the water and honey and stir until thoroughly blended. Stir in the Bénédictine, mandarin purée, and lemon juice; then add the tangerine wedges and lemon wheels. Refrigerate for at least 4 hours to infuse the punch with the flavors of the fruit.

To serve, pour the punch into a punch bowl and add the ice. (Because ice cubes are used for chilling, rather than a large block of ice, the punch will become a bit more diluted than usual over the course of the evening; this is okay.) Ladle into punch glasses or teacups.

NOTE: To make 16 ounces (2 cups) mandarin orange purée, peel and seed 3 mandarin oranges and put the sections in a blender or food processor. Add ½ ounce (1 tablespoon) lemon juice and 1 tablespoon sugar and process until smooth. Strain through a fine-mesh sieve. Stored in a covered container in the refrigerator, the purée will keep for about 4 days. (You can use other types of oranges, but then, of course, it won't be a mandarin orange purée.)

Southern Milk Punch

SERVES 12

TOTAL VOLUME: ABOUT 7 CUPS

**36 ounces (4½ cups)
half-and-half**

**14 ounces (1¾ cups)
brandy, bourbon, or a
combination**

**4 ounces (½ cup)
Tuaca**

¼ cup powdered sugar

**1 teaspoon vanilla
extract**

**Freshly grated nutmeg,
for garnish**

I first tried milk punch in New Orleans, where it's a Sunday brunch staple and every bar and restaurant has its own version, often shaken or blended with ice. For a large group, try this tantalizing rendition, which is frozen to a pleasingly slushy consistency. Although it takes at least three hours to freeze, it can be left in the freezer up to 1 day. Plus, this method doesn't contain added ice, so there's no additional water to dilute the drink. Note that this punch should be served in chilled wine goblets, so plan ahead and put them in the freezer for at least thirty minutes before serving.

In a large bowl that holds at least 8 cups, combine the half-and-half, brandy, Tuaca, powdered sugar, and vanilla and stir until thoroughly blended. Cover and freeze for at least 3 hours, until slightly frozen.

Just before serving, stir the mixture to make it slightly slushy. If it has been sitting in the freezer for longer than 4 hours and is more firmly frozen, use a metal spoon to scrape the top layer into a slush, breaking it up into small pieces. Let sit at room temperature for 30 minutes, stirring occasionally, until the mixture softens to a pourable consistency.

To serve, pour into chilled wine goblets and garnish with a generous grating of nutmeg.

Fish House Punch

28 ounces (3½ cups) hot water

1 cup Demerara sugar

One 750-ml bottle (about 3¼ cups) dark rum

12 ounces (1½ cups) cognac

12 ounces (1½ cups) peach brandy

12 ounces (1½ cups) freshly squeezed lemon juice

1 ice block

Lemon wheels, for garnish

Star anise, for garnish

Many variations of this colonial classic exist, but cocktail historian David Wondrich says this is the most authentic—and I say it's the most delicious. Serve this to celebrate Repeal Day on December 5, the end of that dark time known as Prohibition. Although Wondrich sternly advises against garnishing the drink, the truth is, it looks awfully plain on its own. Repeal Day celebrates rebellion against Prohibition, so go ahead and be a rebel with your garnishes. You can float lemon wheels and star anise in the bowl, as suggested in this recipe. Another option is to garnish each glass with a thin wheel of lemon wrapped around a maraschino cherry, speared with a toothpick to secure.

In a pitcher that holds at least 13 cups, combine the hot water and sugar and stir until the sugar is dissolved. Stir in the rum, cognac, peach brandy, and lemon juice. Cover and refrigerate for at least 3 hours, until thoroughly chilled.

To serve, pour the punch into a punch bowl and add the ice. Garnish with lemon wheels and star anise. Ladle into punch glasses or teacups.

Passyunk Punch

SERVES 10 TO 12
TOTAL VOLUME: ABOUT 6¼ CUPS (WITHOUT ICE)

9 ounces (1 cup plus 2 tablespoons) hot water

4 chai tea bags

6 ounces (¾ cup) honey

16 ounces (2 cups) aged rum (such as Pampero Anniversario)

8 ounces (1 cup) freshly squeezed lemon juice

3 ounces (6 tablespoons) Batavia arrack

2½ teaspoons aromatic bitters (such as Fee Brothers Old Fashion)

8 ounces (1 cup) chilled club soda

1 ice block

2 lemons, sliced into wheels, for garnish

This recipe, named for a neighborhood in South Philly, is from Colin Shearn, manager and bartender at the Franklin Mortgage & Investment Co. in Philadelphia. The secret ingredient is tea. According to Shearn, "tea can help smooth out some of the mistakes you might make in other steps." For example, it can help balance out excessive tartness or sweetness and create more complexity of flavor.

Batavia arrack is an Indonesian spirit distilled from sugarcane and similar to rum. It was a popular ingredient in pre-Prohibition punches, and bartenders love it, but it's still relatively obscure. If you can't find it, some experts recommend substituting a combination of equal parts dark rum and cognac.

In a small bowl, pour 6 ounces (¾ cup) of the hot water over the tea bags and let steep for about 5 minutes. Remove the tea bags, gently pressing to extract the liquid before discarding.

In a punch bowl, combine the honey and remaining 3 ounces (6 tablespoons) hot water and stir until thoroughly blended. Stir in the rum, lemon juice, Batavia arrack, bitters, and steeped tea.

Just before serving, pour in the club soda and stir gently. Add the ice and garnish with the lemon wheels.

To serve, ladle into teacups or small glasses.

The Guild Meeting

SERVES 8
TOTAL VOLUME: ABOUT 8 CUPS (WITHOUT ICE)

30 ounces (3¾ cups) hot water

4 black tea bags (preferably chai or spiced black tea)

½ cup vanilla sugar (see Note)

6 wide strips of orange peel, each about 2 inches long

10 ounces (1¼ cups) freshly squeezed orange juice

10 ounces (1¼ cups) rye whiskey (such as Rittenhouse 100 proof)

4 ounces (½ cup) ginger liqueur (such as Domaine de Canton)

4 ounces (½ cup) Drambuie

4 ounces (½ cup) freshly squeezed lemon juice

1 large ice block or several smaller blocks

This punch recipe was created by Charles Joly, chief mixologist at the Drawing Room in Chicago. Joly's original recipes consistently rack up awards at drink competitions, and this one was a favorite among testers for this book; some even suggested this would be delightful served warm, like a toddy.

In a small bowl, pour the hot water over the tea bags and let steep for about 5 minutes. Remove the tea bags, gently pressing to extract the liquid before discarding.

Put the sugar and orange peel in a punch bowl and muddle lightly to release the oils from the orange peel. Pour in the steeped tea and stir until the sugar is dissolved. Add the orange juice, rye whiskey, ginger liqueur, Drambuie, and lemon juice and stir well. Add the ice.

To serve, ladle into punch glasses or teacups.

NOTE: Although vanilla sugar can be purchased from specialty stores or online, you can also make it by splitting a fresh vanilla bean and burying it in a container of sugar for several days. Or, in a pinch, just add a dash of vanilla extract to regular granulated sugar.

Spiked and Spiced Apple Cider

SERVES 8
TOTAL VOLUME: 6½ CUPS

8 whole allspice berries

10 cinnamon sticks

**32 ounces (4 cups)
apple cider**

**16 ounces (2 cups)
brandy or whiskey**

**4 ounces (½ cup)
honey**

This warming drink, perfect for any autumn gathering, practically calls out for something sweet on the side, like shortbread or apple-cider doughnuts. At home, serve this concoction in a teapot—or just ladle it into mugs straight from the pot on the stove (everyone's probably gathered in the kitchen anyway). Or pour it into a Thermos and take it to a tailgate party to help keep folks' toes warm.

Put the allspice berries and 2 of the cinnamon sticks in a square of cheesecloth and secure with kitchen twine, creating a spice sachet.

In a large saucepan, combine the apple cider, brandy, and honey and stir until thoroughly blended. Add the spice sachet. Cover and bring to a boil over medium-high heat, then lower the heat and simmer, stirring occasionally, for 5 minutes. Remove from the heat and stir again. Discard the spice sachet.

To serve, ladle into glass mugs or footed mugs and garnish each drink with a cinnamon stick.

PITCHER DRINKS

It's an oversimplification to call all the beverages in this section pitcher drinks, since that's only one possible vessel. That said, these cocktails can all be mixed ahead of time (some with a little sparkle added at the last minute) and offered in a pitcher or other container for the host to pour out or for guests to serve themselves. It's up to you how to serve them—perhaps from a sophisticated, curvy carafe for a dinner party, a pitcher for a backyard barbecue, or a large infusion jar for bigger groups. For those with a preference for shaken cocktails (and strong arm muscles), these drinks can be shaken in a large, tightly-capped jar.

SANGRIA 45

SAKE SANGRIA 46

BLOODY MARYS 48

CLASSIC CAIPIRINHAS 49

PIMM'S PITCHER 50

RASPBERRY MOJITOS 52

ROSEMARY REFRESHER 54

MELON MARGARITA MADNESS 56

CEDERBERG COCKTAILS 57

TIPSY PALMER 58

Sangria

SERVES 8
TOTAL VOLUME: ABOUT 7½ CUPS

One 750-ml bottle (about 3¼ cups) red wine (preferably a Spanish wine, such as Rioja)

8 ounces (1 cup) manzanilla sherry

4 ounces (½ cup) orange liqueur (such as Cointreau)

4 ounces (½ cup) freshly squeezed orange juice

1 orange, sliced into wheels

2 lemons, sliced into wheels

1 apple, cored and cut into ½-inch cubes

4 cups ice cubes

Club soda (optional)

It seems as if everyone has a variation on this Spanish stunner, a blend of wine, lots of fruit, and liquor (often brandy, sherry, orange liqueur, or a combination). This drink not only can be but also should be mixed ahead of time to allow the flavors to meld and let the fruit soak up a little boozy goodness. Although I'm calling this a pitcher drink, creative containers are encouraged—this is a drink frequently seen on bartops in infusion jars with spouts.

In a pitcher that holds at least 9 cups, combine the wine, sherry, orange liqueur, orange juice, orange wheels, lemon wheels, and apple cubes and stir well. Cover and refrigerate for at least 1 hour.

To serve, scoop ½ cup ice into each old-fashioned glass and pour in the sangria, spooning some of the booze-soaked fruit into each glass. Top with club soda if desired.

Sake Sangria

SERVES 8
TOTAL VOLUME: ABOUT 7 CUPS

One 720-ml bottle (3 cups) dry sake, chilled

8 ounces (1 cup) cucumber vodka (such as Crop Harvest Earth)

4 ounces (½ cup) ginger liqueur (such as Domaine de Canton)

4 ounces (½ cup) freshly squeezed lemon juice

2 lemons, sliced into wheels

1 cucumber, peeled and sliced into wheels

4 cups ice cubes

Club soda (optional)

White sangrias abound, usually based on white wine. This version, made with dry sake, cucumber-flavored vodka, and ginger liqueur, is crisp and decidedly different. If cucumber-flavored vodka is unavailable, use unflavored vodka and add another slice or two of cucumber to each glass for extra fresh cucumber fragrance.

In a pitcher that holds at least 8 cups, combine the sake, vodka, ginger liqueur, lemon juice, lemon wheels, and cucumber slices and stir well.

To serve, scoop ½ cup ice into large wine tumblers or brandy snifters and pour in the sangria, spooning some of the cucumber and lemon wheels into each glass. Top with club soda, if desired.

Bloody Marys

SERVES 8
TOTAL VOLUME: ABOUT 5 CUPS

**24 ounces (3 cups)
tomato juice**

**12 ounces (1½ cups)
vodka**

**4 ounces (½ cup)
freshly squeezed
lemon juice**

**½ teaspoon
freshly ground pepper**

½ teaspoon celery salt

**½ teaspoon
Worcestershire sauce**

**¼ teaspoon
Tabasco sauce**

Ice cubes

GARNISH BAR
Grated horseradish
Mustard
Celery ribs and/or
cucumber spears
Pickled vegetables
Caper berries
Olives stuffed
with blue cheese
Fresh herb sprigs, such as
basil or cilantro
Lemon and lime wedges
Crisp bacon
Cooked, peeled shrimp

On its own, a basic Bloody Mary is one of the classic brunch drinks. But a DIY Bloody Mary bar, with extra spices and additional garnishes, makes for an interactive and memorable experience. If vodka isn't your thing, feel free to substitute tequila, cachaça, or a smoky mezcal.

In a pitcher that holds at least 6 cups, combine the tomato juice, vodka, lemon juice, pepper, celery salt, Worcestershire, and Tabasco and stir well.

To serve, fill Collins glasses with ice and pour in the cocktail. Garnish as desired.

Classic Caipirinhas

SERVES 8
TOTAL VOLUME: ABOUT 7½ CUPS

6 limes, quartered

½ cup sugar

4 cups crushed ice

16 ounces (2 cups) cachaça

Cachaça, a sugarcane-based spirit, is available at most liquor stores. But if you can't find it, or if you're just inclined to use a different spirit, substitute vodka to create a Caipiroska or rum for a Caipirissima.

In a pitcher that holds at least 9 cups, combine the limes and sugar and muddle until the limes release most of their juices. Stir until the sugar is dissolved. Add the ice and cachaça, and stir again to chill.

To serve, pour the Caipirinhas (including the lime wedges and ice) into old-fashioned glasses.

Pimm's Pitcher

SERVES 8
TOTAL VOLUME: ABOUT 14 CUPS

48 ounces (6 cups) Pimm's No. 1

32 ounces (4 cups) lemon-lime soda

3 cups ice cubes

8 lemon wheels

8 orange wheels

8 cucumber slices

This cool, crisp thirst quencher, which is a natural for summer parties, is a scaled-up version of Pimm's Cup, a classic cocktail made with Pimm's No. 1 and lemon-lime soda. Pimm's No. 1 is an English original, a bittersweet fruit-and-herb-infused gin created by James Pimm in the early 1800s in his London restaurant. It's only 50 proof, so this drink isn't too crazy-strong with the alcohol.

In a pitcher that holds at least 15 cups, combine the Pimm's No. 1 and lemon-lime soda and stir gently until thoroughly combined.

To serve, add the ice and lemon wheels, orange wheels, and cucumber slices; stir gently to chill; then pour into highball glasses. Or, for a neater appearance in the glass, distribute the ice among eight highball glasses; arrange a lemon wheel, orange wheel, and cucumber slice in each glass between the ice and the glass; then pour in the Pimm's mixture.

Raspberry Mojitos

SERVES 8
TOTAL VOLUME: ABOUT 11 CUPS

**8 ounces (1 cup)
freshly squeezed
lime juice**

1 cup superfine sugar

**16 ounces (2 cups)
light rum**

**1⅓ cups fresh
raspberries**

**16 ounces (2 cups)
club soda**

**1 bunch fresh mint,
separated into sprigs**

4 cups ice cubes

Part of this cocktail can be mixed well ahead of party time, but add the club soda and mint leaves just before serving. That way you'll have maximum fizz, along with fresh mint aroma, rather than wilted herbs at the bottom of the pitcher. For plain mojitos, omit the raspberries.

In a pitcher that holds at least 12 cups, combine the lime juice and sugar and stir until the sugar is dissolved. Add the rum and raspberries and stir gently.

Just before serving, pour in the club soda and stir gently. Gently roll the mint between your hands to release the aromatic oils, then add it to the pitcher. Add the ice and stir gently to chill.

To serve, pour into tall glasses, such as Collins glasses, and offer straws.

Rosemary Refresher

16 ounces (2 cups) reposado tequila

12 ounces (1½ cups) freshly squeezed grapefruit juice

6 ounces (¾ cup) Rosemary Simple Syrup (recipe follows)

4 ounces (½ cup) freshly squeezed lime juice

4 cups ice cubes

8 sprigs fresh rosemary, for garnish

This sophisticated margarita variation is a wonderful thirst-quenching aperitif. The recipe makes a bit more rosemary-infused simple syrup than needed for the cocktails. Offer the leftover portion in a small pitcher for anyone who isn't drinking alcohol so they can enjoy it mixed with club soda or ginger ale.

In pitcher that holds at least 10 cups, combine the tequila, grapefruit juice, rosemary syrup, and lime juice and stir until thoroughly blended. Add the ice and stir well to chill.

To serve, pour into old-fashioned glasses and garnish each drink with a rosemary sprig.

Rosemary Simple Syrup

1 cup sugar

8 ounces (1 cup) water

5 sprigs fresh rosemary

In a small saucepan, combine the sugar and water. Cook over medium-high heat, stirring constantly, until the sugar is dissolved. When the syrup starts to boil, lower the heat to maintain a simmer. Gently roll the rosemary between your hands to release the aromatic oils, then add it to the syrup. Cook, stirring occasionally, for 10 minutes. Let cool to room temperature, then remove the rosemary sprigs and strain the syrup if need be. Stored in a covered container in the refrigerator, the syrup will keep for about 2 weeks.

Melon Margarita Madness

SERVES 8
TOTAL VOLUME: ABOUT 9 CUPS

3 cups watermelon, cut into 1-inch pieces and seeded (see Note)

12 ounces (1½ cups) silver tequila

6 ounces (¾ cup) orange liqueur (such as Grand Marnier), plus more as needed

6 ounces (¾ cup) freshly squeezed lime juice

4 cups ice cubes

SALT AND PINK PEPPERCORN RIM (OPTIONAL)

2 tablespoons sea salt

2 tablespoons finely crushed pink peppercorns

Lime wedges

This has to be one of the most refreshing summer cocktails imaginable. It looks especially nice when the glasses are rimmed with the optional pink pepper and salt. More adventurous tipplers might want to try making this with half tequila and half smoky mezcal. However you make it, accompany this drink with tortilla chips and plenty of salsa!

In a food processor or blender, process the watermelon until smooth. Strain through a fine-mesh sieve into a pitcher that holds at least 10 cups. Add the tequila, orange liqueur, and lime juice and stir well. Add the ice and stir again to chill.

Because the sweetness of fresh watermelon can vary, taste before serving and add more orange liqueur, 1 ounce at a time, if needed to achieve the desired sweetness.

To serve, first rim the glasses, if desired. Old-fashioned or margarita glasses are recommended. Combine the salt and peppercorns in a shallow dish and mix well. Run a lime wedge around each glass rim to moisten it, then turn the glass upside down and dip the rim in the salt and pepper mix.

Pour the margaritas into the glasses.

NOTE: When you cut the watermelon into pieces, try to remove as many of the seeds as possible, but don't sweat it; a few seeds won't affect the flavor, and the watermelon is puréed and then strained to remove any fibrous bits.

Cederberg Cocktails

SERVES 8
TOTAL VOLUME: ABOUT 5¼ CUPS

6 ounces (¾ cup) hot water

4 rooibos tea bags

1 cup sugar

12 ounces (1½ cups) Calvados or other dry apple brandy

6 ounces (¾ cup) sweet vermouth (such as Carpano Antica)

6 ounces (¾ cup) freshly squeezed lemon juice

8 dashes Peychaud's bitters

4 dashes Angostura bitters

4 ounces (½ cup) sparkling wine

Ice cubes

1 Granny Smith apple, cored, halved, and sliced into thin half-moons, for garnish

In the name of this recipe, Cederberg refers to the region in South Africa where rooibos tea is grown. This robust, autumnal drink was created by Portland, Oregon, bartender Kelley Swenson, who favors cocktail carafes for smaller groups at dinner parties or backyard gatherings. "You can get really intricate with your recipes," he says, "because you get to prepare them in large batches without the pressure of making drinks *à la minute*."

As is typical for these types of recipes, Swenson calls for adding the sparkling wine right before serving "so the bubbles will bring the cocktail back to life." In addition, he says that for groups larger than eight, "I'd add a splash of sparkling wine to each glass to ensure that guests get the proper effervescence."

In a small bowl, pour the hot water over the tea bags and let steep for 10 minutes. Remove the tea bags, pressing gently to extract the liquid before discarding. Add the sugar and stir until it is dissolved. Let cool to room temperature.

In a pitcher that holds at least 6 cups, combine the steeped tea, Calvados, vermouth, lemon juice, and both bitters and stir well. Cover and refrigerate for at least 2 hours, until chilled.

To serve, pour in the sparkling wine and stir gently. Fill old-fashioned glasses with ice, pour in the cocktail, and garnish with the apple slices.

Tipsy Palmer

SERVES 16 TO 18
TOTAL VOLUME: ABOUT 3½ QUARTS

52 ounces (6½ cups) hot water

10 orange pekoe tea bags (such as Lipton)

One 1-liter bottle (4¼ cups) sweet tea vodka (such as Firefly)

16 ounces (2 cups) freshly squeezed lemon juice

8 ounces (1 cup) Mint Simple Syrup (recipe follows) or Simple Syrup (page 26)

7 to 8 cups ice cubes

16 to 18 fresh mint sprigs, for garnish

16 to 18 lemon wheels, for garnish

A riff on the classic Arnold Palmer, this recipe is courtesy of Stephen Savage, general manager and beverage director at New York City's Tipsy Parson restaurant. Savage serves this in a glass Mason jar—the type used for home canning. To serve it to a crowd, look for a large glass jar with a spigot toward the bottom. For a while, Ball (a canning jar manufacturer) made one-gallon jars like this. If you can find a couple of those, they would be ideal.

In a small bowl, pour the hot water over the tea bags and let steep for about 15 minutes. Remove the tea bags, pressing gently to extract the liquid before discarding. Let cool to room temperature.

Pour the steeped tea into a container that holds at least 6 quarts. Add the vodka, lemon juice, and mint syrup and stir until thoroughly blended. Add the ice and stir well to chill.

To serve, pour into pint canning jars or similar-size glasses and garnish each drink with a sprig of mint and a lemon wheel.

Mint Simple Syrup

1 cup sugar

8 ounces (1 cup) water

1 bunch fresh mint, separated into sprigs

In a small saucepan, combine the sugar and water. Cook over medium-high heat, stirring constantly, until the sugar is dissolved. When the syrup starts to boil, lower the heat to maintain a simmer. Gently roll the mint between your hands to release the aromatic oils, then add it to the syrup. Cook, stirring occasionally, for 10 minutes. Let cool to room temperature, then remove the mint sprigs and strain the syrup if need be. Stored in a covered container in the refrigerator, the syrup will keep for about 2 weeks.

TIKI & TROPICAL DRINKS

Tiki and tropical drinks are some of the most whimsical and fun cocktails around. They are typically spiked with flavors such as pineapple or hibiscus, sweetened with nutty orgeat syrup, and dosed with lots of Caribbean rum, making them guaranteed party pleasers. And they're perfect for this book because many were originally designed as communal libations.

The presentation is part of the fun: Large-volume volcano bowls, scorpion bowls, and tiki-themed footed bowls meant for serving a crowd can be purchased at Polynesian, barware, and party supply shops, or you might get lucky and find tiki mugs at a yard sale. Don't skimp on garnishes, as they will make the presentation more festive. No matter what they're served in, tiki drinks are a wonderful canvas for colorful fruit skewers, edible flowers, teeny umbrellas, and more. Aloha!

Mondo Mai Tai

SERVES 8
TOTAL VOLUME: 4¼ CUPS

16 ounces (2 cups) aged rum (preferably from Martinique, such as Rhum Clément VSOP)

6 ounces (¾ cup) freshly squeezed lime juice

6 ounces (¾ cup) curaçao or orange liqueur

4 ounces (½ cup) dark rum (preferably from Jamaica, such as Appleton Estate Extra)

2 ounces (¼ cup) orgeat syrup

Crushed ice

8 pineapple chunks, for garnish

8 maraschino cherries, for garnish

8 sprigs fresh mint, for garnish

Tiki enthusiasts love to debate who created the mai tai, a perennial tropical favorite. Was it Trader Vic or Don the Beachcomber? It's fun to watch the heated speculation, but only if you already have a cocktail in hand—preferably this one. Since the drink has a relatively somber hue, garnishing lavishly is recommended!

In a glass jar that holds at least 5 cups, combine the aged rum, lime juice, curaçao, dark rum, and orgeat syrup. Cap tightly and shake well. At this point, the cocktail can be refrigerated for up to 8 hours.

To serve, scoop ice into old-fashioned glasses or tiki mugs. Shake the cocktail again, then pour it over the ice. Garnish each drink with a pineapple chunk and cherry skewered on a toothpick accompanied by a sprig of mint.

Zombie

SERVES 8 TO 10
TOTAL VOLUME: 5 CUPS

12 ounces (1½ cups) reposado tequila

8 ounces (1 cup) absinthe

8 ounces (1 cup) pineapple juice

4 ounces (½ cup) passion fruit syrup (such as Monin)

4 ounces (½ cup) freshly squeezed lime juice

4 ounces (½ cup) agave nectar

Crushed ice

4 ounces (½ cup) 151-proof rum (such as Lemon Hart)

8 pineapple wedges, for garnish

This dangerous-sounding drink was made famous by Don the Beachcomber, one of the leading mid-twentieth-century tiki icons, who never revealed his secret recipe. Although this drink usually is rum-based, I tried an unusual tequila-based variation at PKNY (the New York City tiki bar previously known as Pain-killer). This is an adaptation of their version. Beware: This is a strong drink. PKNY allots one per person, with very good reason!

In a pitcher that holds at least 6 cups, combine the tequila, absinthe, pineapple juice, passion fruit syrup, lime juice, and agave nectar and stir until thoroughly blended.

To serve, scoop ice into tiki mugs or tall glasses until three-quarters full, then pour in the cocktail. Finish each drink by floating ½ ounce (1 tablespoon) rum on top (see Note) and garnishing with a pineapple wedge.

NOTE: To float a spirit on top of a drink, hold a metal spoon upside down directly over the drink, with the tip of the spoon against the edge of the glass. Slowly pour the spirit over the back of the spoon so it gently cascades over the spoon and settles on top of the drink. If this is done correctly, the spirit should float on top of the drink in a separate layer.

Hibiscus Rum Cooler

SERVES 8
TOTAL VOLUME: 9½ CUPS

16 ounces (2 cups) dark rum

8 ounces (1 cup) hibiscus syrup

4 ounces (½ cup) freshly squeezed lime juice

4 cups ice cubes

16 ounces (2 cups) ginger beer

The key to this unusual cocktail is hibiscus syrup. I like those made by Fruitlab and Wild Hibiscus, but a number of other brands also offer versions of this rosy-hued, sweet-tart syrup. Although the drink doesn't require a garnish because it has such an attractive color and balanced flavor, consider adorning the serving table with decorative flowers and limes or lime halves.

In a pitcher that holds at least 11 cups, combine the rum, hibiscus syrup, and lime juice and stir until thoroughly blended. Add the ice and stir to chill. Pour in the ginger beer and stir gently.

To serve, pour into tall glasses, such as Collins glasses, and offer straws.

El Diablo

SERVES 8
TOTAL VOLUME: 8¾ CUPS

12 ounces (1½ cups) silver tequila

6 ounces (¾ cup) crème de cassis

4 ounces (½ cup) freshly squeezed lime juice

4 cups ice cubes

16 ounces (2 cups) ginger beer

8 lime wheels, for garnish

El Diablo (Spanish for "the devil") is a classic tiki drink sassed up with ginger beer. Crème de cassis, a liqueur flavored with black currants, imparts an appropriately deep, devilish hue.

In a pitcher that holds at least 10 cups, combine the tequila, crème de cassis, and lime juice and stir until thoroughly blended. Add the ice and stir well to chill. Add the ginger beer and stir gently.

To serve, pour into tall glasses, such as Collins glasses, and garnish with the lime wheels.

Pisco Punch

SERVES 12
TOTAL VOLUME: ABOUT 11½ CUPS (WITHOUT ICE)

One 750-ml bottle (about 3¼ cups) pisco

24 ounces (3 cups) Pineapple Simple Syrup (recipe follows, see Note)

12 ounces (1½ cups) freshly squeezed lemon juice

12 ounces (1½ cups) freshly squeezed lime juice

8 ounces (1 cup) pineapple juice

1¼ ounces (2½ tablespoons) Peychaud's bitters

1 cup pineapple chunks (reserved from simple syrup; see Note)

1 large ice block

Although Pisco Punch isn't a tropical drink, strictly speaking, its light pineapple flavor plus the clove notes of Peychaud's give it a fresh, tropical air. This punch is a San Francisco specialty dating back to the Gold Rush era of the mid-1800s, so its golden hue is fitting. Pisco is a South American brandy distilled from grapes, typically in Peru or Chile. The pineapple syrup must be made at least twelve hours in advance, so plan ahead.

In a large punch bowl, combine the pisco, pineapple syrup, lemon juice, lime juice, pineapple juice, bitters, and pineapple chunks and stir until thoroughly blended. Add the ice.
     To serve, ladle into punch glasses or teacups.

NOTE: You can substitute a pineapple-flavored syrup, such as Monin brand, for the homemade version here. If you do that, replace the reserved pineapple in the punch with an equal amount of fresh or canned pineapple chunks.

Pineapple Simple Syrup

3 cups sugar

12 ounces (1½ cups) water

½ pineapple, cut into 1- to 2-inch chunks

In a small saucepan, combine the sugar and water. Cook over medium-high heat, stirring constantly, until the sugar is dissolved. When the syrup starts to boil, lower the heat to maintain a simmer. Cook, stirring occasionally, for 5 minutes, until slightly thickened. Remove from the heat, add the pineapple chunks, and refrigerate for at least 12 hours. Strain the syrup and reserve the pineapple for the punch. Stored separately in covered containers in the refrigerator, the syrup will keep for about 1 week, and the pineapple will keep for about 2 days.

Eureka Tiki Punch

20 ounces (2½ cups)
honey

20 ounces (2½ cups)
water

60 ounces (7½ cups)
light-bodied aged
amber rum (such
as Appleton Estate
Reserve)

60 ounces (7½ cups)
freshly squeezed
lemon juice

20 ounces (2½ cups)
Yellow Chartreuse

8 ounces (1 cup)
ice water

1 tablespoon
plus ¾ teaspoon
Angostura bitters

80 ounces (10 cups)
ginger ale (such as
Fever-Tree)

1 large ice block or
several smaller blocks

Lemon wheels,
for garnish

Fresh mint sprigs,
for garnish

Edible flowers,
for garnish

SERVES 40
TOTAL VOLUME: ABOUT 8½ QUARTS (WITHOUT ICE)

The recipe for this tiki party crowd-pleaser (and I do mean a crowd!) is courtesy of Martin Cate, owner of Smuggler's Cove in San Francisco. This can be served in several bowls placed throughout a party area or one enormous vessel.

In a small saucepan, combine the honey and water and cook over low heat, stirring constantly, until thoroughly blended. Let cool to room temperature.

In a container that holds at least 9 quarts, combine the honey mixture, rum, lemon juice, Chartreuse, water, and bitters and stir until thoroughly blended. Cover and chill for at least 2 hours.

To serve, pour the mixture into one or more punch bowls. Pour in the ginger ale and stir gently. Add the ice and garnish with lemon wheels, mint sprigs, and edible flowers. Ladle into tiki mugs.

NOTE: Want to set this baby on fire? Here's Martin Cate's recommended technique: You'll need a 1-inch square of white bread, left out to dry overnight. Soak the bread in lemon extract, then place it in a hollowed-out lime hull. Float the lime hull in the punch and use a long match or lighter to set it on fire. This will create a dramatic tall yellow flame. Just be sure to have a pitcher of water and tongs on hand! If the bread starts to blacken and smell like toast, grab it with the tongs and dunk it in the water to extinguish the flame.

Scorpion Bowl

SERVES 8
TOTAL VOLUME: ABOUT 11 CUPS

18 ounces (2¼ cups) light rum

18 ounces (2¼ cups) freshly squeezed orange juice

12 ounces (1½ cups) freshly squeezed lemon juice

4 ounces (½ cup) orgeat syrup

3 ounces (6 tablespoons) brandy

4 cups ice cubes

Crushed ice

Gardenia flowers, for garnish (optional)

This is a classic communal libation—never drink a Scorpion Bowl alone! Serve this in several small bowls, each for two or three people, or in a larger bowl for a group. Although classic vessels labeled "scorpion bowls" or "volcano bowls" can be purchased at barware or party supply stores, let your imagination run wild here. I've even seen this drink served in a large fishbowl. Just don't forget the long straws—essential for sharing!

In a pitcher that holds at least 8 cups, combine the rum, orange juice, lemon juice, orgeat syrup, and brandy and stir until thoroughly blended. Working in batches if need be, combine the mixture with the ice cubes in a blender and process until slushy.

To serve, scoop crushed ice into one or more scorpion bowls or other vessels and pour in the cocktail. Garnish with a gardenia flower, if desired, and provide a long straw for each imbiber.

Piña Coladas

SERVES 8
TOTAL VOLUME: ABOUT 10 CUPS

**16 ounces (2 cups)
light rum (preferably
from Puerto Rico)**

**16 ounces (2 cups)
cream of coconut (such
as Coco López)**

**16 ounces (2 cups)
pineapple juice**

4 cups ice cubes

**8 pineapple wedges
(optional), for garnish**

**8 maraschino cherries,
for garnish**

Serve this festive tropical drink in coconut halves, hollowed-out pineapples, or tiki mugs if you have 'em. If not, tall Collins glasses work well, too.

In a pitcher that holds at least 7 cups, combine the rum, cream of coconut, and pineapple juice and stir well. Working in batches if need be, combine the mixture with the ice and process in a blender until slushy.

To serve, pour into tiki mugs or Collins glasses and garnish each drink with a pineapple wedge, if desired, and cherry speared on a toothpick.

COCKTAIL MATH NOTE: This recipe is easy to scale up or down; just use 2 ounces (¼ cup) each of rum, cream of coconut, and pineapple juice, plus about ½ cup of crushed ice per serving.

Classic Daiquiris

SERVES 8
TOTAL VOLUME: 3 CUPS

**12 ounces (1½ cups)
white rum**

**6 ounces (¾ cup)
freshly squeezed
lime juice**

**6 ounces (¾ cup)
Simple Syrup (page 26)**

SUGARED RIM (OPTIONAL)

**¼ cup sugar, or as
needed**

Lime wedges

Ice cubes

**8 lime wheels,
for garnish**

As the story goes, this classic cocktail was created in Cuba and named in honor of the nearby village of Daiquiri.

In a pitcher that holds at least 4 cups, combine the rum, lime juice, and simple syrup and stir until thoroughly blended.

To serve, first rim the glasses, if desired. Margarita glasses are recommended. Put the sugar in a shallow dish. Run a lime wedge around each glass rim to moisten it, then turn the glass upside down and dip the rim in the sugar.

Stir the rum mixture with a long-handled spoon. For each two drinks, pour 6 ounces (¾ cup) of the mixture into a mixing glass with ice. Stir well to chill, then strain into two Margarita glasses and garnish each drink with a lime wheel.

COCKTAIL MATH NOTE: The formula for this cocktail is quite straightforward and easy to scale for large groups. Just remember that the ratio is two parts rum to one part each lime juice and simple syrup.

Frozen Strawberry-Basil Daiquiris

SERVES 8
TOTAL VOLUME: ABOUT 12 CUPS

4 cups strawberries, hulled

12 ounces (1½ cups) white rum

6 ounces (¾ cup) freshly squeezed lime juice

6 ounces (¾ cup) Simple Syrup (page 26)

4 ounces (½ cup) orange liqueur

¾ cup fresh basil leaves, lightly packed, plus 8 sprigs fresh basil, for garnish (optional)

4 cups ice cubes

There's nothing like a round of strawberry daiquiris for a beach party, and a blender makes this a snap to prepare for groups. Chilled glasses are highly recommended for this cocktail, so you'll need to plan ahead and put them in the freezer for at least thirty minutes before serving.

Cut four of the strawberries in half for the garnish and set aside. Coarsely chop the remaining strawberries.

In a pitcher that holds at least 4½ cups, combine the rum, lime juice, simple syrup, and orange liqueur and stir until thoroughly blended. Working in batches if need be, combine the rum mixture, chopped strawberries, basil leaves, and ice in a blender and process until smooth.

To serve, pour into chilled Margarita glasses and garnish each drink with a sprig of basil, if desired, and a strawberry half.

Northshore Cocktails

SERVES 8
TOTAL VOLUME: 2½ CUPS

6 ounces (¾ cup) whiskey with a peaty, smoky flavor profile (such as Peat Monster)

6 ounces (¾ cup) almond syrup or orgeat syrup (such as Monin)

4 ounces (½ cup) hibiscus liqueur (such as Hum)

4 ounces (½ cup) freshly squeezed lime juice

Ice cubes

8 strips of lemon peel, for garnish

This pleasingly fruity yet smoky cocktail, created by Arizona mixologist Jason Asher, is an unorthodox but delicious addition to the tiki canon.

In a pitcher that holds at least 3 cups, combine the whiskey, almond syrup, hibiscus liqueur, and lime juice and stir until thoroughly blended.

To serve, scoop ice into old-fashioned glasses and pour in the cocktail. Garnish each drink with a strip of lemon peel.

Suffering Bastard

SERVES 8
TOTAL VOLUME: 7 CUPS

32 ounces (4 cups) ginger ale

8 ounces (1 cup) bourbon

8 ounces (1 cup) gin

8 ounces (1 cup) freshly squeezed lime juice

4 or 5 dashes Angostura bitters

Crushed ice

8 maraschino cherries, for garnish

8 orange wedges, for garnish

8 sprigs fresh mint, for garnish

Legend has it that this drink was invented in the 1940s in Cairo and was originally named the Suffering Bar Steward. Presumably, too many drinks led to its new, slurred pronunciation. Some tiki bars gleefully serve variations on this drink with the name gleefully morphed from Suffering to Dead, Dying, or even Inglorious Bastard.

In a pitcher that holds at least 8 cups, combine the ginger ale, bourbon, gin, lime juice, and bitters and stir gently until well combined.

To serve, scoop ice into tiki mugs or highball glasses and pour in the cocktail. Garnish each drink with a cherry and orange wedge skewered on a toothpick alongside a sprig of mint.

COOL & CLASSIC DRINKS

The wonderful drinks in this chapter are classics for a reason—but they were created to be mixed painstakingly, one by one. Now, these drinks have been adapted for serving to larger groups.

Here's how it works: All the ingredients are decanted into a clean bottle, then cold water is added to approximate the effect of melting ice. When a cocktail is shaken with ice, the volume of the liquid typically increases by about 25 percent as the ice fragments and melts into the drink. That said, with some of the cocktails in this chapter, I found that adding 10 to 20 percent water hit the sweet spot.

Sure, you could simply chill premixed drinks without adding water, but the flavor won't be the same as what you expect from the classic versions of these cocktails. A bit of dilution softens the taste and balances the drink. For optimum flavor, serve bottled cocktails as cold as possible, and shake them well before pouring, especially if citrus, sugar, or a syrup is part of the drink, since those ingredients tend to separate.

Madison Avenue Manhattans

SERVES 8
TOTAL VOLUME: 3½ CUPS

16 ounces (2 cups) rye whiskey

8 ounces (1 cup) sweet vermouth (such as Carpano Antica)

4 ounces (½ cup) water

1 teaspoon Angostura bitters

8 Brandied Cherries (page 23), for garnish (optional)

My buddy Nora has a passion for classic cocktails and retro entertainment, so it was only a matter of time before she threw a party with a *Mad Men* theme. Guests were invited to come in retro attire, and we partied like it was 1965.

Nora mixed up a pitcher of Manhattans using a recipe along these lines, with spicy rye whiskey, and then funneled the cocktails back into an empty liquor bottle, which made for easy pouring—even while wearing proper white gloves.

In a pitcher that holds at least 4 cups, combine the whiskey, vermouth, water, and bitters and stir well. Using a funnel, decant into a 1-liter liquor bottle or two 750-ml liquor bottles. Cap tightly and refrigerate for at least 2 hours, until chilled.

To serve, set out a bowl or wine bucket filled with ice. Shake the bottle to ensure the cocktail is well mixed, then set it in the ice so it stays chilled. Pour into coupe glasses and garnish each drink with a cherry, if desired.

COCKTAIL MATH NOTE: To scale this drink up or down, it's a simple two-to-one ratio, two parts rye to one part vermouth, plus a half part water. Use ⅛ teaspoon bitters per drink.

Bobby Burns

SERVES 8
TOTAL VOLUME: ABOUT 4 CUPS

**12 ounces (1½ cups)
Scotch**

**12 ounces (1½ cups)
sweet vermouth (such
as Carpano Antica)**

**5 ounces (½ cup plus
2 tablespoons) water**

**2 ounces (¼ cup)
Bénédictine**

**8 lemon twists,
for garnish**

Looking for an excuse to chase away the late-January blahs? Celebrate Burns Night on January 25. This drink—perfect for Scotch lovers—is named for famed Scottish poet Robert Burns, who wrote "Auld Lang Syne." Since this drink is essentially all spirits (with no juice or mixers), traditionally it would be stirred rather than shaken. The method here, for making a bottled version, deviates from that rule, but it's effective for serving a large group. It's also rather strong!

In a pitcher that holds at least 5 cups, combine the Scotch, vermouth, water, and Bénédictine and stir well. Using a funnel, decant into a 1-liter liquor bottle or two 750-ml liquor bottles. Cap tightly and refrigerate for at least 2 hours, until chilled.

To serve, set out a bowl or wine bucket filled with ice. Shake the bottle to ensure the cocktail is well mixed, then set it in the ice so it stays chilled. Pour into coupe or martini glasses and garnish each drink with a lemon twist.

COCKTAIL MATH NOTES: The Scotch and vermouth are poured in equal parts, with just one-sixth part of Bénédictine. That formula makes it easy to mix up the cocktail in any size batch. And with a few small variations, you can make a number of other Scotch-based drinks using similar formulas. Here are some examples:

· ROB ROY: 2 parts Scotch and 1 part sweet vermouth, with a couple of dashes of Angostura bitters per drink, served on the rocks in old-fashioned glasses, garnished with a maraschino cherry.

· RUSTY NAIL: Equal parts Scotch and Drambuie, stirred with ice and served in old-fashioned glasses (some variations call for a little more Scotch than Drambuie).

· LOCH NESS: 1½ parts Scotch, 1 part Pernod, and ¼ part sweet vermouth, stirred with ice in old-fashioned glasses.

Blood and Sand

SERVES 8
TOTAL VOLUME: 3½ CUPS

8 ounces (1 cup) Scotch

8 ounces (1 cup) freshly squeezed orange juice

6 ounces (¾ cup) cherry liqueur (such as Heering)

6 ounces (¾ cup) sweet vermouth (such as Carpano Antica)

Ice cubes

Named after the 1922 silent-screen romance starring Rudolph Valentino, this classic was originally made with equal amounts of its four ingredients. While that makes for a nicely straightforward formula, most people seem to prefer this cocktail with the sweetness dialed down a little, as reflected in this recipe. This cocktail is the ideal quaff for a movie marathon, especially if the films feature the Latin Lover. By the way, this drink also can be served bottled (add 6 ounces [¾ cup] cold water) or on the rocks.

In a pitcher that holds at least 4 cups, combine the Scotch, orange juice, cherry liqueur, and vermouth and stir well.

To serve, stir well with a long-handled spoon. For each two drinks, pour 7 ounces (¾ cup plus 2 tablespoons) of the mixture into a mixing glass with ice. Stir well to chill, then strain into two martini glasses.

Japanese Cocktails

SERVES 8
TOTAL VOLUME: ABOUT 3 CUPS

16 ounces (2 cups) cognac

4 ounces (½ cup) orgeat syrup

2 ounces (¼ cup) water

½ ounce (1 tablespoon) Angostura bitters

8 lemon twists, for garnish

Classic cocktail buffs will recognize this drink as a "Professor" Jerry Thomas original, circa 1860. The drink contains no Asian ingredients; rather, according to legend it was created by Thomas to honor the arrival of the first Japanese delegation to visit the United States.

Using a funnel, decant the cognac, orgeat syrup, water, and bitters into a bottle that holds at least 3 cups, such as a 750-ml liquor bottle. Cap tightly, shake, and refrigerate for at least 2 hours, until chilled.

To serve, set out a bowl or wine bucket filled with ice. Shake the bottle to ensure the cocktail is well mixed, then set it in the ice so it stays chilled. Shake the bottle well before pouring the cocktail into martini glasses. Garnish each drink with a lemon twist.

Aviation Cocktails

SERVES 8
TOTAL VOLUME: ABOUT 4 CUPS

16 ounces (2 cups) dry gin (such as Aviation)

6 ounces (¾ cup) maraschino liqueur (such as Luxardo)

6 ounces (¾ cup) freshly squeezed lemon juice

2½ ounces (5 tablespoons) water

8 Brandied Cherries (page 23), for garnish

This crisp, classic cocktail speaks of the era surrounding Prohibition. It was created by New York bartender Hugo Ensslin at the Wallick Hotel in the early twentieth century, and the recipe was published in *The Savoy Cocktail Book* by Harry Craddock, one of the most famous barmen of the 1920s and 1930s. Craddock—who created a number of beloved cocktail classics—often is credited with the Aviation, too, but we know better, don't we?

In a pitcher that holds at least 5 cups, combine the gin, maraschino liqueur, lemon juice, and water and stir well. Using a funnel, decant into a 1-liter liquor bottle or two 750-ml liquor bottles. Cap tightly and refrigerate for at least 2 hours, until chilled.

To serve, set out a bowl or wine bucket filled with ice. Shake the bottle to ensure the cocktail is well mixed, then set it in the ice so it stays chilled. Because citrus juice tends to separate from spirits, shake the bottle well before pouring the cocktail into coupe or martini glasses. Garnish each drink with a cherry.

Vodka Gimlets

SERVES 8
TOTAL VOLUME: 2¾ CUPS

16 ounces (2 cups) vodka

6 ounces (¾ cup) lime cordial

Ice cubes

8 lime wheels, for garnish

The secret to a great gimlet is a great lime cordial. In a pinch, lime juice mixed with simple syrup or agave nectar can be substituted, but it's worth making your own. This recipe makes more lime cordial than needed for the cocktails. Offer some of the leftover portion in a small pitcher for designated drivers to splash into ginger beer or tonic water. If you like, you can substitute gin for the vodka.

Using a funnel, decant the vodka and lime cordial into a bottle that holds at least 2¾ cups, such as a 750-ml liquor bottle. Cap tightly, shake well, and refrigerate for at least 2 hours, until chilled.
     To serve, set out a bowl or wine bucket filled with ice. Shake the bottle to ensure the cocktail is well mixed, then set it in the ice so it stays chilled (gimlets are best when served as cold as possible). Fill old-fashioned glasses halfway with ice. Shake the bottle well before pouring in the cocktail. Garnish each drink with a lime wheel.

Lime Cordial

28 ounces (3½ cups) water

1 cup sugar

4 ounces (½ cup) freshly squeezed lime juice

In a small saucepan, combine the water and sugar. Cook over medium-high heat, stirring constantly, until the sugar is dissolved. Let cool to room temperature. Stir in the lime juice. Cover and refrigerate until chilled, about 3 hours. Stored in a covered container in the refrigerator, the lime cordial will keep for about 1 week.

Cosmopolitans

SERVES 8
TOTAL VOLUME: 4½ CUPS (WITHOUT ICE)

Ice cubes

16 ounces (2 cups) lemon vodka (such as Absolut Citron)

8 ounces (1 cup) orange liqueur (such as Cointreau)

8 ounces (1 cup) cranberry juice

4 ounces (½ cup) freshly squeezed lime juice

8 lime wedges, for garnish

Any bachelorette party or "girls' night in" deserves a pitcher of festive Cosmos, a fruity cousin to the martini. Carrie Bradshaw would approve! Note that this cocktail should be served in chilled martini glasses, so plan ahead and put them in the freezer for at least thirty minutes before serving.

Scoop some ice into a pitcher that holds at least 8 cups. Add the vodka, orange liqueur, cranberry juice, and lime juice and stir well to chill.

To serve, carefully strain into chilled martini glasses, making sure no ice gets into the glasses. Garnish each drink with a lime wedge.

Silver Screen Martinis

SERVES 8
TOTAL VOLUME: 2½ CUPS (WITHOUT ICE)

Ice cubes

16 ounces (2 cups) gin

4 ounces (½ cup) dry vermouth (such as Vya or Dolin Blanc)

GARNISH BAR

Green olives and/or stuffed olives (see page 24)

Juice from the olives (in a squeeze bottle or small pitcher), for dirty martinis

Cocktail onions (see page 24), for Gibsons, and/or pickled vegetables

Sprigs of fresh herbs, such as basil, presented in a glass or vase

Citrus twists (see page 26)

Orange bitters and other light-flavored bitters (such as Fee Brothers cranberry or celery)

Dry vermouth (some people prefer equal amounts gin and vermouth, which is known as a Fifty-Fifty)

The martini is a straightforward drink, and a natural accompaniment to a marathon of black-and-white film classics. Of course, those films often feature martinis, including *The Thin Man* (1934), in which detective Nick Charles offers some advice on how to mix drinks. "Always have rhythm in your shaking. Now a Manhattan you always shake to fox-trot time, a Bronx to two-step time, a dry martini you always shake to waltz time." Never mind that these cocktails are all actually better stirred; it's still a great scene.

In this recipe, what turns the cocktail into a party is a DIY garnish bar. Provide a variety of extras, and your guests will create some pretty snazzy drinks. Note that this cocktail should be served in chilled martini glasses, so plan ahead and put them in the freezer for at least thirty minutes before serving.

Scoop some ice into a pitcher that holds at least 5 cups. Add the gin and vermouth and stir well to chill.

To serve, carefully strain into chilled martini glasses, making sure no ice gets into the glasses. Garnish as desired.

Negronis

SERVES 8 TO 10
TOTAL VOLUME: ABOUT 2¾ CUPS

6 ounces (¾ cup) gin

6 ounces (¾ cup) Campari

6 ounces (¾ cup) sweet vermouth (such as Carpano Antica)

3½ ounces (7 tablespoons) water

8 to 10 wide strips of orange peel or orange half wheels, for garnish

It is said that every bartender eventually has an affair with the Negroni. Maybe it's the alluring bittersweet profile, or maybe it's the striking rosy hue. This recipe is for a bottled version served straight up. However, this cocktail is frequently served on the rocks. For a rocks version, omit the water.

In a pitcher that holds at least 4 cups, combine the gin, Campari, vermouth, and water and stir well. Using a funnel, decant into a bottle that holds at least 2¾ cups, such as a 750-ml liquor bottle. Cap tightly and refrigerate for at least 2 hours, until chilled.

To serve, set out a bowl or wine bucket filled with ice. Shake the bottle to ensure the cocktail is well mixed, then set it in the ice so it stays chilled. Pour into coupe or martini glasses and garnish each drink with a strip of orange peel.

The Last Word

SERVES 8
TOTAL VOLUME: 3½ CUPS

6 ounces (¾ cup) gin

6 ounces (¾ cup) Green Chartreuse

6 ounces (¾ cup) maraschino liqueur (such as Luxardo)

6 ounces (¾ cup) freshly squeezed lime juice

4 ounces (½ cup) water

8 lime wheels, for garnish

If you're not familiar with the Last Word, ask any bartender about it. This potent Prohibition-era cocktail, made with equal parts gin, lime juice, Green Chartreuse, and maraschino liqueur, is seriously beloved in mixology circles.

Using a funnel, decant the gin, Green Chartreuse, maraschino liqueur, lime juice, and water into a bottle that holds at least 3¼ cups; a 750-ml liquor bottle will just fit this amount. Cap tightly, shake, and refrigerate for at least 2 hours, until chilled.
     To serve, set out a bowl or wine bucket filled with ice. Shake the bottle to ensure the cocktail is well mixed, then set it in the ice so it stays chilled. Because citrus juice tends to separate from spirits, shake the bottle well before pouring the cocktail into coupe glasses. Garnish each drink with a lime wheel.

INDEX

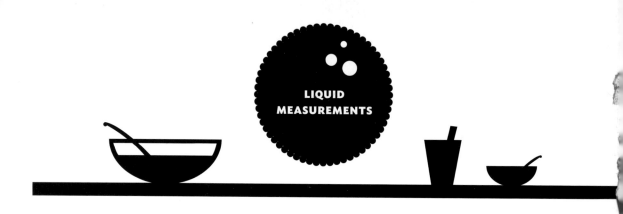

LIQUID MEASUREMENTS

U.S.	METRIC
$\frac{1}{4}$ cup (4 tbsp)	60 ml
$\frac{1}{3}$ cup (5 tbsp)	75 ml
$\frac{3}{8}$ cup (6 tbsp)	90 ml
$\frac{1}{2}$ cup (8 tbsp)	120 ml
$\frac{5}{8}$ cup (10 tbsp)	150 ml
$\frac{2}{3}$ cup (11 tbsp)	165 ml
$\frac{3}{4}$ cup (12 tbsp)	180 ml
$\frac{7}{8}$ cup (14 tbsp)	210 ml
1 cup (16 tbsp)	240 ml
2 cups (1 pt)	480 ml
4 cups (1 qt)	960 ml
8 cups (2 qt)	2 L